# ISOLATION
## VS.
# INTERVENTION

## Is America the World's Police Force?

Karen Bornemann Spies

*Twenty-First Century Books*

**A Division of Henry Holt and Company**
**New York**

Twenty-First Century Books
A division of Henry Holt and Company, Inc.
115 West 18th Street
New York, New York 10011

Henry Holt® and colophon are registered trademarks of Henry Holt and Company, Inc.
*Publishers since 1866*

Published in Canada by Fitzhenry & Whiteside Ltd.
195 Allstate Parkway, Markham, Ontario L3R 4T8

Printed in the United States of America

Created and produced in association with Blackbirch Graphics, Inc.

Series Editor: Tanya Lee Stone

**Library of Congress Cataloging-in-Publication Data**

Spies, Karen Bornemann.
    Isolation v. intervention: is America the world's police force? / Karen Bornemann Spies. — 1st ed.
        p.    cm. — (Issues of our time)
    Includes bibliographical references and index.
    Summary: Discusses isolationism and intervention both as philosophies and with reference to major historical events including the World Wars, the Cold War, Haiti, and Bosnia.
    ISBN 0-8050-3880-9 (acid-free paper)
    1. United States—Foreign relations—Juvenile literature.  2. Intervention (International law)—Juvenile literature. 3. Neutrality—United States—History—Juvenile literature. [1. United States—Foreign relations. 2. Intervention (International law). 3. Neutrality.] I. Title. II. Series.
E183.7.S68   1995
327.73—dc20                                                          95-19444
                                                                              CIP
                                                                              AC

# Contents

# 1

......

# Isolation and Intervention

**H**ow involved should the United States be in the affairs of other countries?  When, if ever, should this country:

- declare war?
- bring "democracy" to other countries?
- donate food and medical supplies to nations fighting civil wars?
- have colonies overseas?
- send troops to other nations—or sell those nations weapons?

Our nation has struggled with questions such as these since its settlement.  At various times in America's history, our leaders have reacted to such questions in a variety of ways.

During times of conflict, people often have different viewpoints as to whether or not the United States should be involved.  Here, people protest the Gulf War in an anti-war demonstration in November 1990.

People on one side of the issue say that America should take care of its own needs first and avoid involvement in the political or economic affairs of other nations. They feel that nations should solve their own housing and medical problems. The U.S. government should focus on solving America's problems, not those of other countries. This viewpoint is known as "isolationism."

People on the other side of the issue support a viewpoint called "interventionism." Interventionists believe that the United States has a duty to serve as the world's leader and to supply military and economic aid to other countries. They believe the United States should enter wars to defend what they consider threats to American lives and property. Interventionists think we cannot ignore the political, economic, and social situations in other nations.

## Offensive Intervention

Intervention is most often considered "offensive," or aggressive. Offensive intervention is what occurs when a government intentionally becomes involved in the affairs of another nation without provocation. War is the ultimate offensive intervention. Beginning with the American Revolution, the United States has been involved in a number of wars. A desire for additional territory caused the United States to declare war on Mexico in 1846. The United States intervened in Cuba and the Philippine Islands during the Spanish-American War. The Korean War and Vietnam War are both examples of offensive American intervention that have occurred in the past fifty years.

Beginning in colonial times, many Americans have considered it the nation's unique duty to spread democracy. Thomas Paine, writing in *Common Sense,* said, "We have it in our power to begin the world again."

Thomas Paine believed in America's capability and responsibility to spread democracy.

Religious reasons have also been given to support American intervention. In 1850, Herman Melville stated, "We Americans are the peculiar, chosen people—the Israel of our time; we bear the ark of the liberties of the world. . . . God has predestined. . . the rest of nations must be in our rear."

American presidents have also developed political statements to support intervention. In 1823, President James Monroe told Congress, "The American continents . . . are henceforth not to be considered as subjects for future colonization by any European powers." This statement became known as the Monroe Doctrine. President John Tyler used this doctrine to justify seizing Texas in 1842.

## Defensive Intervention

At other times in America's history, the nation has intervened "defensively" by intervening only after another nation has acted first against the United States. One type of response, economic intervention, takes the form of trade agreements with other nations and trade embargoes (restrictions) to protect America's interest. In February 1995, the United States said that it would impose a 100 percent surcharge (fee) on goods imported from China to discourage the Chinese from continuing to copy American computer software, books, movies, and recordings without permission. China agreed to change its policies to avoid the tariffs.

The United States has sometimes claimed that military force was used for defensive reasons, such as to protect resources. In 1991, under President George Bush, U.S. forces attacked Iraq for its invasion of Kuwait. Much of the oil used in America was produced in Kuwait. One reason given for the attack was to safeguard American oil resources.

U.S. military force has also been used to protect the lives of Americans who were in danger. In 1983, Communists took over the Caribbean island of Grenada. President Ronald Reagan sent troops to rescue American students who were studying medicine there and became trapped.

Another reason given for using military force is to protect nations who are American allies. For example, troops were sent to help South Korea when Communist North Korea attacked in 1950.

America's military might has been used for humanitarian reasons. Great Britain and the United States airlifted food, clothing, fuel, and medicine to West Berlin after the Soviets blockaded the city in 1948.

America's entrance into the Gulf War was described as defensive based on the threat of America's oil resources being in jeopardy. Here, members of a U.S. ground crew wave to a U.S. F-16 fighter plane in support for a safe mission.

### Reasons Against Intervention

As a young nation, the United States followed isolationist policies. President George Washington warned that the United States should have "as little political connection as possible" with foreign nations. President Thomas Jefferson feared "entangling alliances" with Europe.

The fear of becoming involved in other nations' wars has persisted. In 1940, the America First Committee was organized to oppose American involvement in World War II. Protesters against the Vietnam War helped bring about America's withdrawal from Southeast Asia.

This tradition of noninvolvement is based on a number of factors. A major argument against military intervention is that it is extremely costly, in both material and lives. The war in Vietnam cost over $140 billion. More than 57,000 Americans died from battle wounds, disease, and other causes. The Desert Storm attacks on Iraq in 1991 cost American taxpayers approximately $60 billion.

Members of the America First Committee attend an anti-war rally in May 1941. Famous pilot Charles Lindbergh (seated second from left) was a key spokesman for this organization.

By intervening, Americans deny other nations their right to choose their own form of government. Many feel that forcing our form of government on another nation only demonstrates a lack of understanding of that nation's culture. Daniel Yankelovich, a political polltaker, asserts that "Americans feel unqualifiedly that this is the best

country in the world. . . .
The dark side of this attitude
is that we don't believe we
can be wrong . . . . We're
not looking at the world
from anybody else's point
of view."

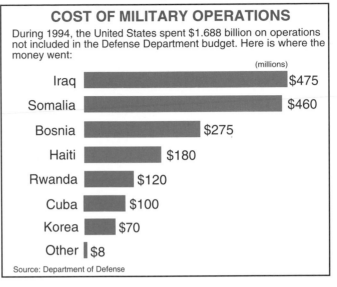

**COST OF MILITARY OPERATIONS**

During 1994, the United States spent $1.688 billion on operations not included in the Defense Department budget. Here is where the money went:

(millions)

| | |
|---|---|
| Iraq | $475 |
| Somalia | $460 |
| Bosnia | $275 |
| Haiti | $180 |
| Rwanda | $120 |
| Cuba | $100 |
| Korea | $70 |
| Other | $8 |

Source: Department of Defense

Such a viewpoint may lead
to resentment against our
country. For example, be-
tween 1904 and 1935, the
United States interfered in the affairs of many Latin
American nations, causing negative feelings that
linger to the present time.

If intervention is not carefully planned or if it
goes awry, the United States looks inept. President
Jimmy Carter sent troops to Iraq in 1979 to rescue
American hostages. The failure of the mission
lowered America's prestige overseas and damaged
President Carter's reelection campaign.

Even a major world power like the United States
cannot become involved in every dispute in the
world. There are too many problems to be solved.
We literally do not have enough time, money, or
resources to become involved, even if we wanted to,
in every issue or crisis. How, then, does America
decide if and when to become involved? Should the
United States serve as the world's police force?

# 2
·······

# From Isolation to Intervention and Back Again

**F**rom the earliest days of our nation's history, we have leaned toward isolationism. The first European settlers came to America to escape hardship, religious persecution, and European wars. The long ocean voyage emphasized the New World's separateness from Europe. That separation was not only geographic; the people who came here thought of themselves as a different culture.

But during the American Revolution, the colonies had no navy, little money, and few trained army officers. In order to have any chance of defeating Great Britain, they needed a powerful ally. They turned to France for help.

A scene from the Boston Massacre in 1770. Although early colonists tended to be isolationists, America's need for assistance from France during the American Revolution marked the beginning of foreign "entanglements."

After the Revolution, the United States could not remain isolated. Problems with European countries plagued the new nation. The British would not give up their forts along the Canadian border. The Spanish disputed the southern border of the United States.

In 1793, Great Britain and France went to war. The French expected support from America in return for French aid during the Revolution. But war with Britain would destroy the American economy. About three-quarters of the country's trade was with her former parent. In April 1793, President Washington issued a Proclamation of Neutrality in which he refused to take sides in conflicts occurring between other powers.

Washington then used diplomacy to reach peaceful solutions. With Jay's Treaty of 1794, the British agreed to withdraw from their forts, and trade was resumed. The following year, disputes with Spain were solved with the signing of the Pinckney Treaty.

In his Farewell Address in September 1796, Washington warned against favoring the interest of one nation over another. He said, "Europe has a set of primary interests which to us have a very remote relation . . . It is our true policy to steer clear of permanent alliances with any portion of the foreign world, so far, I mean, as we are now at liberty to do it." American leaders since that time have used Washington's statement to justify isolationism.

Thomas Jefferson, our third president, while acquiring new territory for the United States, still hoped to avoid intervention. But disputes with both France and Great Britain prevented America from remaining isolated. Napoleon Bonaparte threatened to establish a French empire in the Louisiana Territory. But the French colony of St. Domingue (present-day Haiti) rebelled and Napoleon's troops were gravely reduced. Napoleon then gave up his plans for an empire in Louisiana and sold the territory to the United States for $15 million.

In 1803, Great Britain and France again went to war. The United States could hardly remain neutral after the British "impressed" (kidnapped) American sailors from U.S. vessels and forced them to serve on British ships.

The impressment of American seamen by the British was an initial cause of the United States entering the War of 1812.

Yet, President Jefferson refused to intervene with military force. Instead, he asked Congress to forbid American ships from entering foreign ports so the British could not seize American sailors. Congress responded with the Embargo Act, which ended up harming American trade. The United States lost the major markets for its goods.

Americans were growing tired of being bullied by the British. Many new young leaders were elected to Congress in 1812. Known as "war hawks," they pushed for war with Great Britain. Americans felt their honor had to be defended.

As a result of the War of 1812, the young nation gained international attention. The American navy performed well, and Andrew Jackson won an important battle at New Orleans. America proved it could defend itself against a powerful nation.

### The Monroe Doctrine Warns Against Intervention

After the war, the United States entered a period known as "the era of good feeling." Nationalism (a feeling of devotion to one's country) swept the nation. Nationalistic feelings at home influenced how the American government acted toward other nations. When Spain's colonies in Latin America declared independence between 1814 and 1824, the United States issued the Monroe Doctrine, under the

administration of President James Monroe, to show support. This document warned European nations to keep out of the Western Hemisphere. In turn, the United States pledged to stay out of European affairs.

This 1912 painting by Clyde de Land illustrates the creating of the Monroe Doctrine. James Monroe is shown standing.

## Manifest Destiny
## Encourages Expansion

By the 1840s, a spirit of expansionism filled the nation. John O'Sullivan, a writer and editor, wrote that it was "our manifest destiny to overspread and to possess the whole continent which Providence has given us." Manifest destiny fueled the desire for an American harbor on the Pacific coast. The term was used by "expansionists," those who wanted the United States to acquire more territory.

In the 1820s, Mexico gained independence from Spain and encouraged foreigners to settle in what is now the state of Texas. By 1830, so many Americans had come that Mexico began to limit their numbers. These new Texans wanted the rights and freedoms they had enjoyed in America, so they rebelled in 1836. Sam Houston and his armies won independence, and the United States annexed (took control of) Texas in 1845.

The border between Texas and Mexico remained under dispute and Mexico broke off diplomatic relations with the United States. In April 1846, Mexican and American troops met in a minor battle. President James Polk used the skirmish as a reason to declare war. A large number of Americans agreed with Polk. Writers such as James Fenimore Cooper and Walt Whitman described how war fulfilled America's destiny to spread democracy.

But other Americans considered the Mexican War an unfair attack on a weaker nation. Some members of Congress, including Abraham Lincoln, questioned whether Polk had even attempted to avoid war.

## Interventionism Declines Again

After the Mexican War, the United States stretched from coast to coast. But some Americans still were not satisfied. Cuba's rich sugar plantations were particularly attractive, so in

1848, the United States offered Spain $100 million for the island. Spain refused to sell and, in secret, American diplomats plotted to obtain Cuba. They drew up an agreement called the Ostend Manifesto. It stated that if Spain would not sell Cuba, the United States would take it by force. The American public was stunned to learn about the agreement. Protests against it were so strong that the government gave up the idea.

Lincoln opposed slavery and, during the Civil War, slavery threatened to break up the nation. The Gettysburg Address, given in November 1863, expressed Lincoln's opinion that nations "conceived in liberty" should not perish.

By the 1850s, the United States had little time to spend in the affairs of other nations. Slavery and other sectional issues threatened to break apart the Union. President Abraham Lincoln, in his Gettysburg Address, said that the United States was "a nation conceived in liberty and dedicated to the proposition that all men are created equal." Many people, in Europe and Latin America as well as the United States, felt that the United States was a model of democracy. They agreed with Lincoln's statement that America was the "last best hope" of democracy. The Civil War threatened to destroy the nation. However, the United States did remain one nation. And in the next century, America became a world leader.

# 3
∙ ∙ ∙ ∙ ∙ ∙

# America:
# A World Power

**A**fter the Civil War ended in 1865, America faced many changes. The South had to rebuild, while the North continued to grow as an industrial center. Americans constructed railroads across the continent and settled the Great Plains.

## The Nation Expands

In the process of settling the plains, the United States intervened strongly in the lives of the Native Americans who lived there. The U.S. government signed hundreds of treaties with the various tribes, but often failed to carry out the agreements. To defend their way of life, the Native Americans attacked the

A strong interventionist, Theodore Roosevelt and his cavalry of Rough Riders went to the aid of the Cuban people in the Spanish-American War.

settlers and the railroads. The U.S. government sent troops to forcibly move the people to reservations (areas of land set aside by the government).

Between 1860 and 1880, the United States focused more on internal growth than on international relations. But the nation did intervene in several situations. In 1867, Napoleon III tried to set up an empire in Mexico. But America, calling upon the Monroe Doctrine, sent 50,000 soldiers to the Mexican border. The French forces quickly withdrew.

By the 1880s, the United States had become the world's leading industrial nation. The positive feelings filling the country helped change the way Americans looked at their relationships with other nations. Up to this point, the nation had grown by expanding through North America. Expansionists felt that the United States should now build a colonial empire like France, Germany, and Japan were doing. Colonies would provide the thriving U.S. economy with additional markets for its goods and bases where merchant ships could refuel.

The desire to build a colonial empire is called imperialism. Leaders who supported imperialism included naval historian Alfred Thayer Mahan, Senator Henry Cabot Lodge, and Theodore Roosevelt. Key elements of imperialism included creating a strong navy and building a canal through Central America. Naval and merchant ships could use the canal to easily move between oceans. Imperialists also wanted to obtain military bases and new markets for trade in the Pacific and Latin America.

The Spanish-American War signaled a major shift in U.S. foreign policy toward intervention. In 1895, Cubans rebelled against their Spanish colonial rulers. President William McKinley hoped to remain neutral. But he cautioned that if the Spanish military continued to mistreat Cuban citizens, the United States would intervene.

Alfred Mahan was an influential American who advocated imperialism. His ideas were used to promote building the Panama Canal and naval bases in Hawaii, the Philippines, and other Pacific territories.

The incident of the U.S. battleship *Maine* made war with Spain a certainty. Early in 1898, while on a friendly visit, the *Maine* exploded in the Havana harbor, killing 260 Americans. Most Americans assumed the Spanish were responsible. "Remember the *Maine*" became the rallying cry for war.

When further negotiations with the Spanish failed, President McKinley asked Congress to declare war. The declaration of war included the Teller Amendment, which stated that the United States would not annex Cuba. Expansionists were disappointed about the amendment. But humanitarian forces in the U.S. Congress insisted that control of the island be returned to Cuba as soon as the war ended.

### Annexing the Philippines

To interventionists, the Spanish-American War offered an opportunity to gain a base in the Pacific. Spain had a small naval squadron based at Manila in the Philippines. In May 1898, Commodore George Dewey sank the Spanish warships before they could leave the harbor and American troops quickly occupied Manila. When the Spanish surrendered, however, the United States did not give control of the islands back to the Philippines. President William McKinley decided it was America's job to "educate the Filipinos, and uplift and civilize and Christianize them, and by God's grace, do the very best we could by them, as our fellow men for whom Christ died." Taking over the Philippines forced the United States into another war. The Filipinos rebelled against the United States but were defeated three years later.

To many Americans, battling the Filipinos seemed contrary to the idea of freedom and self-government. In 1916, the United States agreed to eventually grant independence to the Philippines. However, this promise was not fulfilled until thirty years later.

## "Speak Softly and Carry a Big Stick"

When Theodore Roosevelt became president in 1901, American foreign policy became strongly interventionist. Roosevelt believed America should "speak softly and carry a big stick." Under his leadership, Puerto Rico became a U.S. territory and Cuba became a "protectorate," a region under the control of a stronger nation.

Roosevelt's most controversial action was obtaining the Panama Canal zone in 1903. He supported a revolt in Panama and the United States immediately recognized Panama's independence. Roosevelt bragged, "I took the canal zone."

A number of Latin American nations experienced financial problems during Roosevelt's terms. In 1902, Venezuela refused to pay its debts to Great Britain and France. In 1904, the Dominican Republic declared bankruptcy. Roosevelt was concerned that European nations might use force to collect these debts. Because he viewed such intervention as a violation of the Monroe Doctrine, he announced a new interventionist policy in 1905 known as the "Roosevelt Corollary." It stated that America would become "an international police power" in the Western Hemisphere and intervene whenever nations in that hemisphere demonstrated "chronic wrong-doing." Many presidents have used the Roosevelt Corollary to support U.S. intervention

The acquisition of the Panama Canal was a subject of controversy. Here, Secretary Leslie Shaw signs the largest warrant ever issued by the U.S. treasury at that time.

in the Dominican Republic, Cuba, Nicaragua, Mexico, the Panama Canal, and Haiti. But it has caused a legacy of resentment toward the United States that continues to this day.

By expanding overseas, America appeared to be abandoning its earlier policy of isolationism. Yet this was not entirely the case. The United States had not made any commitments or alliances with foreign nations.

## Dollar Diplomacy

President William Howard Taft, who succeeded Roosevelt, advocated "dollar diplomacy." He maintained that his foreign policy was "substituting dollars for bullets." He urged private American investment to bring economic growth to Latin America and China. Taft also felt that the U.S. government should protect American investments overseas. In 1909, he had the U.S. government purchase the debts of Honduras in an effort to gain control of that Latin American nation. In Nicaragua, he intervened economically and also militarily. Taft took over Nicaragua's debts to European banks and sent marines to help overthrow one government and support the establishment of another. However, little money was invested through dollar diplomacy and resentment against U.S. intervention increased. Critics—then and now—felt that the policy resulted in excessive interference in foreign governments.

## Isolationism
## Returns

In 1913, President Woodrow Wilson succeeded Taft. He vowed to return American foreign policy to its roots. Wilson opposed expanding into foreign territories and forcing economic controls on other nations. He wanted foreign policy decisions to be based on human rights.

U.S. Marines were deployed to Mexico in 1914 to lend aid in a fight for human rights. The troops, however, were unwanted and were attacked by the rebels they aimed to assist.

President Wilson was instrumental in creating the peace treaty that ended World War I. He is shown seated on the far right.

But events outside of President's Wilson's control forced him into intervention. In 1914, he sent U.S. Marines to support a rebellion in Mexico. But the rebels did not want help and they rioted against the U.S. troops.

Problems also brewed overseas. Europe was filled with strong nationalistic feelings and had built up their military forces. Military alliances formed, increasing tensions. The world exploded in a struggle—the likes of which had never before been experienced.

President Wilson hoped that the United States could remain neutral, calling the conflict "a war with which we had nothing to do." But Germany began an all-out submarine war against American shipping vessels. In April 1917, President Wilson asked Congress to declare war to "make the world safe for democracy." America's entrance into World War I helped to bring about an end to the fighting on November 11, 1918.

Wilson led the American delegation to the Paris Peace Conference after World War I. He envisioned the world community settling differences in an international organization called the League of Nations. The Covenant of the League of Nations was incorporated into the Treaty of Versailles, which ended the war.

But Americans were not ready for such a broad alliance. The Senate refused to ratify the Treaty of Versailles. Wilson suffered a stroke in 1919. He recovered by 1920, but was unable to work out any compromise with the Senate.

Before 1914, the United States had developed into a great world power. After the war, however, many Americans wanted a return to "normalcy." The mood of the nation had once again changed back to one of isolationism.

# 4
······

# World War II and the Cold War

After World War I, the nation's focus turned inward. President Warren G. Harding's campaign, "a return to normalcy," offered people the promise that the United States would return to life the way it had been before the war.

However, the nation was too involved in international affairs to remain isolated. Both Presidents Harding and Coolidge followed the Roosevelt Corollary, sending troops to the Caribbean to "preserve order." The marine occupation of the Dominican Republic, which started in 1904, continued through both the Harding and Coolidge administrations. In 1926, Coolidge sent 5,000 marines to help put down a revolt against Nicaraguan president Adolfo Diaz. Marine occupation forces, which

After the Japanese attacked Pearl Harbor in 1941, America had no hope of remaining neutral in World War II. Here, U.S. troops move toward Paris the day after the liberation of the French capital in 1944.

werc originally sent in 1915 to put down a revolt against the government, remained in Haiti until 1935.

Americans were becoming aware of the resentment Latin American nations felt toward them. President Herbert Hoover worked to build goodwill with a "Good Neighbor" policy. Shortly after taking office, he visited ten Latin American countries and later stopped U.S. military intervention in Latin America. Under Franklin D. Roosevelt, this policy continued.

## Depression
### Leads to War
Economic disaster struck much of the world during the 1930s. While the United States struggled to overcome the Great Depression, economic problems in Europe led to government takeovers by dictators. Leaders such as Adolf Hitler in Germany and Benito Mussolini in Italy took control and promised to bring prosperity to their countries.

War broke out in Europe in 1939. Americans questioned U.S. involvement. Isolationists wanted to put "America First" and let the remainder of the world handle its own problems. Internationalists felt America's safety was directly related to Europe's ability to defeat Hitler and the Axis powers. Therefore, Great Britain and the Allies needed U.S. military aid to win. However, this position risked drawing America into the war.

In 1937, Roosevelt warned, "There is no escape through mere isolation or neutrality." He maintained that the United States must be "the arsenal of democracy." By 1940, America was selling the Allies as many weapons as they could afford.

When European funds ran low, the U.S. Congress passed a "lend-lease" loan program, which authorized the president to give supplies to American allies. The supplies could be lent on any terms the president felt would protect American security. When the United States began shipping the supplies to Europe, German U-boats (submarines) attacked the merchant ships carrying the lend-lease materials. Roosevelt ordered the U.S. Navy to shoot back.

The Japanese attack on Pearl Harbor in December 1941 ended any American hopes for neutrality. After Germany was defeated in 1945, the United States and its allies combined to defeat Japan.

On March 11, 1941, President Franklin D. Roosevelt signed the lend-lease bill that would aid Great Britain.

Nagasaki was the second city to feel the fury of the atomic bomb when Truman authorized it to be dropped there on August 9, 1945.

Harry S. Truman became president after Roosevelt's death in April 1945. Truman authorized dropping atomic bombs on the Japanese cities of Hiroshima and Nagasaki. Following this, the Japanese government surrendered.

The destruction that was caused by this terrible weapon focused American foreign policy in a different direction. After World War I, the United States had isolated itself from Europe's affairs and avoided responsibility for keeping the peace worldwide. But the experiences of World War II proved that such a position was impossible. The threat of nuclear destruction made a third world war something that must be avoided. The United States developed a foreign policy designed to prevent such a catastrophic "hot war."

## The Beginnings
## of the Cold War
Just before the end of World War II, the United Nations (UN) was formed as a world peacekeeping body. The United States joined immediately. Americans now realized that the nations of the world needed to work together to make peace a reality.

But as soon as the war ended, the Allies no longer had a common enemy. They disagreed on post-war plans for Central and Eastern Europe. The United States and Great Britain wanted each European country to choose its own political system. The Soviet Union pursued communism, in which only one political group, the Communist party, ran the government. It owned and controlled all the property and the entire economic system of the Soviet Union.

Joseph Stalin, the leader of the Soviet Union, took control of Hungary and other Eastern European nations. He refused to allow free elections. Prime Minister Winston Churchill of Great Britain accused Stalin of closing off the Soviet Union behind an "iron curtain."

From 1945 to 1989, U.S. foreign policy aimed at breaking down the iron curtain and preventing the spread of communism. This policy, which President Truman stated in the Truman Doctrine, was known as containment. Congress supported this policy by

Writer Walter Lippmann gained fame for his book entitled *The Cold War*. The title of his book coined the phrase that is still used to describe America's strained relationship with the Soviet Union following World War II.

voting $400 million to aid Greece and Turkey. The Greek government was battling a Communist takeover. If Greece fell to Communist control, Turkey, its neighbor, might soon follow.

Some Americans felt containment was not aggressive enough. They called for all-out military action to stop the Communists from taking over additional territory. Others felt such action was an invitation for a third world war. Writer and editor Walter Lippmann felt containment set a dangerous precedent. It required the United States to defend every anti-Communist government, even those headed by harsh dictators. Lippmann explained his views in a book called *The Cold War*. Its title was quickly used to describe the relationship between the United States and the Soviet Union after World War II.

### The Marshall Plan
In June 1947, Secretary of State George C. Marshall proposed the European Recovery Program. Under the Marshall Plan, the United States would provide money, machinery, and supplies. Although western European nations welcomed the plan, the Soviet Union and her satellites (Soviet-controlled nations) refused to participate. The Soviets said it was an attempt to force nations to accept capitalism (an economic philosophy based on private ownership of business).

## NATO (North Atlantic Treaty Organization)

The nations of western Europe feared Soviet expansion. In 1949, twelve of them asked the United States to join them in the North Atlantic Treaty Organization (NATO). The treaty stated that if a member nation was attacked, the other members would consider it an attack on them. This arrangement for mutual defense was called collective security.

U.S. involvement in NATO was a giant step away from isolationism. NATO was the first "entangling alliance" the United States had formed since the Revolutionary War, when it signed an alliance with France in 1778. In addition, it was the first time in its history that the United States had agreed to a peacetime defense of Europe.

Ceremonies were held for the signing of NATO on April 4, 1949. Shown signing the agreement in this picture is Ambassador Tarchiani of Italy.

## Decisions
## in Asia

After World War II, the Chinese Communists and Nationalists resumed their civil war. The United States intervened, using diplomacy to try to resolve the fighting. When these efforts failed, the Nationalists asked for military assistance. The United States decided it was more important to use America's limited funds to help the recovery in Europe than to fight communism in China.

In 1949, the Communists defeated the Nationalists, who fled to Taiwan. Many Americans criticized the government for "losing China" to Communist leadership. Senator Robert A. Taft said that state department leaders had "surrendered to every demand of the Soviet Union and promoted, at every opportunity, the Communist cause in China."

After the Japanese surrender in World War II, Soviet troops occupied Korea north of the 38th parallel (latitude) and established a Communist government there. On June 25, 1950, North Korea invaded South Korea. When the North Koreans refused to withdraw, the United Nations sent in forces under U.S. General Douglas MacArthur.

President Truman ordered U.S. military troops to Korea to fight Communists without asking Congress to declare war. Sending American troops to Korea was controversial, since the war was supposed to be a UN effort. But America furnished the majority of the troops and supplies. More than 45,000 U.S. soldiers lost their lives in this supposed UN action.

A second source of controversy related to Truman's aggressive move in sending American military troops to Korea. He did this without asking Congress to declare war. Truman maintained that he was acting properly under his authority as the commander-in-chief. However, many observers considered his action unconstitutional.

The conduct of the war caused further conflict about U.S. intervention in the area. In addition to defeating North Korea, General MacArthur wanted to bomb mainland China and restore the Nationalists to power. Truman feared such action would lead to war with China. He relieved MacArthur of his command. The U.S. Congress investigated the dismissal and approved Truman's action.

Six months prior to Truman's dismissal of General MacArthur, Truman is shown here admiring the medal of merit he presented to MacArthur for outstanding performance in the field.

In the meantime, fighting went on in Korea. Truce talks finally began in July 1951, after Dwight D. Eisenhower became president. In 1953, a cease-fire was declared. Korea was left divided, as it had been before the war. Because of the huge loss of lives, many Americans questioned whether or not the intervention was justified.

After achieving a cease-fire in Korea, Eisenhower faced a new challenge in Vietnam. The French, at war with the Vietnamese, wanted the United States to bomb Communist strongholds. Eisenhower feared that if the United States did not intervene, the Communists might take over all of Southeast Asia. He compared the situation to a row of dominoes. If the first is knocked over, the others will follow. But Congress refused to support U.S. intervention in Vietnam. The French withdrew, and a dividing line at the 17th parallel was chosen to separate Communist North Vietnam from South Vietnam.

President Eisenhower involved the United States in a number of covert, or secret, interventions. He used the Central Intelligence Agency (CIA) to overthrow unfriendly governments in Iran (1953) and Guatemala (1954). He sent surveillance planes to spy on Russia. In 1960, one of these U-2s was shot down, causing embarrassment for the United States.

The Eisenhower Doctrine signaled America's intent to intervene in the Middle East. He asked

Congress to give the president the right to use force to defend any Middle Eastern country that asked for help against Communists. In 1957, the doctrine was used to justify sending troops to Lebanon.

The cold war "heated up" with the building of the Berlin Wall in 1961. The new Soviet leader Nikita Khruschev ordered the wall built in order to prevent Germans from leaving Communist-controlled East Germany. The wall was a visible sign that the Soviet Union intended to keep tight control of Eastern Europe.

West Berliners watched East German laborers erect a concrete wall on August 23, 1961. The Berlin Wall divided East and West Berlin for the next twenty-eight years.

# 5
.......

# The Bay of Pigs to Bosnia

When President John F. Kennedy took office in January 1961, he learned that the CIA had been training Cuban exiles (refugees) for an invasion of Cuba. On April 17, 1961, a force of about 2,000 landed at the Bay of Pigs and tried to overthrow Fidel Castro's Communist government. Within two days, Castro's soldiers had killed or captured all the invaders. The CIA had predicted that the Cuban people would rise up and rebel against Castro, but such a rebellion never took place. Kennedy took full blame for the failure.

But Kennedy intervened successfully during the Cuban Missile Crisis. In October 1962, he announced that he had received intelligence reports showing that Soviet nuclear missiles

Through Operation Restore Hope, the United States participated in a humanitarian intervention and brought food and assistance to the Somalis in 1992.

U.S. intervention became necessary during the Cuban Missile Crisis in 1962, as Soviet missiles based in Cuba were used to threaten America. President Kennedy (shown with arm extended) was successful in his efforts to thwart a war.

had been set up in Cuba. The missiles were aimed at the United States. If fired, they could destroy the eastern two thirds of the country in less than five minutes.

Kennedy established a naval blockade to prevent delivery of additional missiles to Cuba and insisted that the Soviets remove the missiles already there. After several days of tense negotiations, carried on partly in secret, the Soviets agreed to withdraw the missiles. The United States then promised not to invade Cuba and war was prevented.

### The Vietnam War

The seeds of later protest over the Vietnam War were sown during Kennedy's administration. Since 1954, the United States had supported the authoritarian government in South Vietnam. During the spring of 1963, its leader, Ngo Dinh Diem, began to persecute Buddhists living in South Vietnam, causing many Americans to protest. Nevertheless, Kennedy increased support to the

South Vietnamese government in response to increased Communist North Vietnamese military aid to rebels in South Vietnam. Kennedy also sent military "advisers" to South Vietnam. In September 1963, he still said of the people of South Vietnam that, "In the final analysis, it is their war. They are the ones who have to win it or lose it. We can help them, we can give them equipment, we can send our men out there as advisers, but they have to win it...."

What further steps Kennedy might have taken will never be known. He was assassinated in Dallas, Texas, on November 22, 1963.

The Vietnam War dominated the presidency of Kennedy's successor Lyndon B. Johnson. At the time President Johnson took office, there were no American ground troops in Vietnam and only 23,000 advisers. By the end of the war, however, Johnson had sent 575,000 soldiers to Vietnam.

The more he increased American involvement in the war, the more Americans protested. He ordered bombing of North Vietnam in February 1965, after the Viet Cong (Communist rebels fighting in South Vietnam) attacked an American military camp. Within a month, the bombing had increased far beyond paying back any attacks on American soldiers. With each attack, the Communists' guerrillas (jungle fighters) increased their efforts. In turn, Johnson stepped up American military action.

Protests against the war increased when Americans learned Johnson had kept many facts about the war secret. In August 1964, he ordered bombing raids of North Vietnam in response to their attacks of American destroyers in the Gulf of Tonkin. A later Senate investigation showed that the order to strike back was prepared long before the Gulf of Tonkin incident. Many Americans believed Johnson had deliberately prompted the North Vietnamese to attack just to have an excuse to attack them.

The Johnson administration insisted the war was not a civil war. Rather, it represented the threat of a total Communist takeover of the rest of the world. By 1967, however, many respected leaders, such as Senators Mike Mansfield and Robert Kennedy, had joined the side of Americans protesting U.S. involvement. Critics said that U.S. intervention in Vietnam did not help spread democracy, since the rulers of South Vietnam were corrupt and lacked the support of their own people.

Many other nations also deplored U.S. involvement in the war. They criticized America for setting itself up as a judge of what was best for people. Because the American government spent so much time and effort on the Vietnam War, little energy was left to devote to other world problems.

Due to public opinion against the war, Johnson announced in March 1968, that he would not run for

Much of the American public was vehemently against American involvement in the Vietnam War. Here, a group of anti-war protesters demonstrate their cause.

reelection.  Never before had so much military might been used in such an unsuccessful war. Johnson's actions in Vietnam had moved the mood of the American public toward anger, frustration, and isolationism.

## Strong
## Foreign Policy    Richard Nixon took office in 1969, and quickly intervened in Southeast Asia, despite public opinion against further involvement. He secretly planned the bombing of Cambodia and increased involvement in Vietnam, even though his election campaign included promises to end the war. The *New York Times* called Nixon's saturation bombing of North Vietnam "diplomacy through terror."  In 1972, he also sent troops to invade Laos.

As anti-war protests continued, President Nixon succeeded in obtaining a cease-fire in Vietnam in January 1973.  By the end of March, all American troops had withdrawn. More than 57,000 Americans died in Vietnam and more than 300,000 were wounded—without banishing communism. At least one million Southeast Asians were killed or wounded.

The Vietnam War had caused terrible damage to America's prestige and its view of itself as a world leader. In 1976, the year Jimmy Carter was elected president, the nation celebrated its bicentennial and questioned whether or not its 200-year-old values were valid. Some critics felt that America had become too bold and arrogant in pursuing wars such as Vietnam. Others questioned whether or not the United States truly had a right to its exceptional prosperity. They suggested America's leadership should instead be aimed at preserving its resources and sharing its wealth with other nations.

With the election of Ronald Reagan in 1980, America entered a new period of optimism about its world leadership. Reagan restored confidence by improving the economy and cutting government spending. His popularity encouraged him to take a strong role in foreign affairs; as a result, the United States pursued a strongly anti-Communist, interventionist stand. In Nicaragua, the Reagan administration, through the government of Iran, sent money and supplies to the contras (rebels trying to overthrow the Communist government). The Reagan administration involved Iran in an effort to strengthen

A sign painted on a wall in Grenada in November 1983, expresses sentiments that the American presence in Grenada was appreciated when U.S. forces led an invasion to overthrow the Communist government.

America's relationship with that government. Although Congress passed laws forbidding such use of military assistance, several of Reagan's aides secretly continued funding the contras. The resulting scandal became known as the "Iran-contra affair."

In October 1983, Reagan sent military forces to Grenada in the Caribbean with great success. The United States rescued 800 American medical students and overthrew the Communist government there.

In 1988, Reagan's vice president George Bush was elected president. Bush continued the aggressive intervention policies of the Reagan administration.

He ordered an invasion of Panama to capture and remove dictator Manuel Noriega from power. A U.S. grand jury had indicted, or accused, Noriega of dealing in drugs.

Bush also intervened decisively in the Gulf War. On August 2, 1990, Iraq invaded Kuwait, violating the UN charter. Bush created an alliance of twenty-five countries, including nations from Europe and the Middle East. When efforts at diplomacy failed, Bush obtained congressional approval to attack. A series of massive air strikes and a powerful land campaign quickly destroyed Iraq's once-strong army.

### The End of the Cold War Has Far-Reaching Impact
When Mikhail Gorbachev became Soviet Premier in March 1985, relations between America and the Soviet Union began to relax. Gorbachev introduced the concept of *glasnost*, a new openness in Soviet society. Other members of the Communist party were "hardliners" who feared Gorbachev's ideas. They took control of the government in 1991. Russian president Boris Yeltsin led the Russian people against the new government. Other republics soon demanded independence. By 1992, the Soviet Union no longer existed.

Since the end of World War II, decisions about whether or not to intervene in the affairs of other nations were mainly based on considering how the Soviets would react. With the absence of this giant enemy, the United States must now rethink how it reacts to other nations, including the fifteen new Soviet republics.

This task faced President Bill Clinton when he took office in 1992. His actions have had mixed results. In September 1994, Clinton intervened in Haiti to try to restore the first democratically elected president—Jean-Bertrand Aristide—and correct human rights violations. An American invasion force was on its way when Haiti's military leaders agreed to leave the island.

In other foreign interventions, Clinton has been less decisive. In Somalia, civil war left many citizens starving and homeless. Through Operation Restore Hope, troops brought food and supplies to the starving Somalis. President Clinton then decided to send 400 U.S. Rangers to capture General Mohammed Farrah Aidid, a warlord dictator, but the mission failed. Debate continues over what the United States' role should be in Somalia.

The situation in Bosnia presented yet another challenge. Muslim Serbs waging civil war in the Balkan nation destroyed much of the republic. By March 1995, a costly 24,000-member UN peacekeeping force had been unable to halt the battling. Of Bosnia, Clinton has said, "You can't allow the mass extermination of people and just sit by and watch it happen." But the president and his advisers continue to debate what action, if any, the United States should take, or if it should support UN intervention in the area.

Unrest in the Korean peninsula presented another challenge to Clinton. North Korea's leader Kim Il Sung threatened to use force to unite North and South Korea under North Korean leadership by 1995. North Korea possesses a well-equipped military force, a stockpile of chemical weapons, and, according to secret CIA reports, probably one or two atomic weapons. In April 1995, Clinton threatened to destroy North Korea if that nation used nuclear weapons. At the same time, he pushed for

American citizens have differing opinions on U.S. involvement in Bosnia. This demonstration oustide the White House in February 1993 supports intervention for humanitarian reasons.

# Jimmy Carter

As our thirty-ninth president, Jimmy Carter felt America should be "right and honest and truthful and decent" in dealing with other nations. He intervened with economic sanctions (restrictions), diplomacy, and military force to work toward peace and human rights. In 1980, to protest the Soviet invasion of Afghanistan, Carter announced that the United States would boycott the Olympic Games held in Moscow. He also established a grain and trade embargo against the Soviet Union. In 1979, he arranged the first peace treaty between Israel and Arab nations but failed to rescue American hostages in Iran.

The hostage crisis doomed Carter's chances for re-election in 1980, but did not stop his involvement in foreign affairs. In 1986, the Carter Center of Emory University was founded, which works toward solving international disputes. He has personally intervened to try to find a solution to conflicts that the U.S. government has been unable to resolve.

In June 1994, Carter arranged an agreement with North Korea to allow inspection of their nuclear reactor by outsiders. The following September, Carter went on a peace mission to Haiti with Senator Sam Nunn and former chairman of the joint chiefs of staff Colin Powell. They convinced dictator Raoul Cédras to withdraw from Haiti. Carter has also gone to Bosnia to meet with Serbian leaders in hopes of resolving the civil war there. Of his peacekeeping missions, the former president states, "I hope that some of my efforts for peace and human rights will be remembered."

continued talks with North Korea about making its nuclear sites available for inspection by a neutral force such as the United Nations.

If North Korea used nuclear or chemical weapons to attack South Korea, would the United States use military force to defend its ally, South Korea? Clinton and his advisers would have to decide whether or not the threat of nuclear destruction or possible world war would be worth the further loss of American life in Korea.

# 6

# Where Do We Go From Here?

**W**ithout the threat of Soviet aggression, the United States now must form a new foreign policy. As the only superpower left, should America try to police the actions of other countries? To what extent should the United States provide humanitarian aid to nations in distress?

Total isolation is not possible. Communications capabilities have increased because of satellite, cable, and cellular technology. Every nation knows what every other nation is doing, or can soon find out.

The economies of the world are intertwined. Banks and other businesses have offices worldwide. The United States has money invested in foreign banks and companies, which, in turn,

Many Americans feel strongly that the United States has enough serious problems on the homefront and that the U.S. government should focus more on national crises.

own property and businesses in the United States. In addition, the United States has borrowed money from foreign banks, giving these banks some control over the American economy.

Perhaps the opposite of isolation is not aggressive direct intervention but, instead, continuous engagement. In other words, maybe the United States should seek to maintain constant contact with both friendly and less friendly nations. Disputes can be worked out through diplomacy.

But eventually contact may break down. Then the United States will have to choose when and how to intervene. The first step is to consider whether or not taking action would be in the best interests of the nation. But what is our national interest? Not all politicians and citizens agree. Public opinion supported American involvement in the Gulf War. But when the United States took steps toward invading Haiti in 1994, public opinion was divided.

Maintaining the safety and security of the Western Hemisphere is of vital interest to the United States. Many people who objected to our involvement in the Vietnam War did so

**KEEPING THE PEACE**

Where the United States had the most troops deployed in 1994.

Source: Department of Defense

because they felt that Americans were dying in a distant land for no purpose directly related to America's safety. Becoming involved in a civil war in Bosnia appears to prompt similar objections.

The question of the president's role in intervention must be clarified. Congress has the power to declare war, but the president is the commander-in-chief of the armed forces. Bush obtained congressional approval to begin the Gulf War; Reagan did not when he attacked Grenada.

President Bush's administration attacked Iraq and liberated Kuwait in the Gulf War, after deciding that vital oil resources were at stake.

One reason given by presidents who act on their own is that their decision was made to save Americans. Acting quickly may, in fact, have this result. On the other hand, such action is potentially unconstitutional and gives one person too much power.

## Making Decisions on Intervention

George Bush said, "In the complex new world we are entering, there can be no simple set of fixed rules for using force. Inevitably, the question of military intervention requires judgment. Each and every case is different." The following list of criteria to consider is a compilation of suggestions made by several people, including President Clinton, George Bush, Richard Nixon, and political writers Michael Kramer, Richard J.

Barnet, and John Cavanagh, and UN ambassador Madeleine Albright. They are to:

• Use force as a last resort.

Because of the threat of nuclear disaster, diplomacy should be exhausted before war is declared.

• Follow through on commitments.

If the United States promises to use force in a particular situation, then we must follow through. Otherwise, our credibility is ruined.

• Have a clearly stated goal.

The mission in Grenada was clear: to eliminate Communist control and rescue Americans. Our goal in Vietnam was not as focused.

Humanitarian reasons for intervention are probably the most easily understood by a majority of citizens. Here, an American marine offers a helping hand to a young Somali boy in Mogadishu in 1993.

• Have a high probability of public support.

• Compare the means to the ends.

Government leaders must consider the possible cost in lives and materials before engaging in war.

• Intervene for the right reasons.

Intervening to correct human rights violations is likely to be supported by many. Taking over another country for selfish reasons is not.

• Consider cultures and relationships.

Intervention in Latin America caused resentment toward the United States. Much of the unrest in the former Soviet republics is the result of deep-seated hatreds or religious differences. It may be impossible for an outside source such as the United States to truly understand or solve such differences. Intervention may cause additional conflict as well as generate resentment against the United States for interfering.

The same experts also offer alternatives to forceful intervention. In determining our foreign policy for the future, the United States could consider additional ways to intervene nonmilitarily. Options could include:
• Taking a leadership role in peacekeeping ventures.
• Encouraging free trade and economic conditions worldwide.

Instead of sending soldiers, America could provide technical advisers to distribute information on free trade and help other countries improve their industrial technology.
• Developing a worldwide environmental protection program.

Should America serve as the world's police force? Each conflict or situation must be examined individually. Sometimes, as in the past, America may choose to become involved. At other times, the United States may decide that intervention is not in the best interests of the American people or the world as a whole.

# Glossary

**annex**  The process of adding territory to an existing nation.

**collective security**  An association of nations that agree to take action whenever the national security of any member nation is threatened.

**communism**  A totalitarian form of government in which one political party has total control of the government and the means of industrial production.

**containment**  The policy or result of preventing the expansion of communism.

**expansionism**  A national policy of seeking to increase the size of a nation's territory.

**imperialism**  The philosophy or practice of a nation increasing its power by acquiring territory by peaceful or aggressive means.

**internationalism**  A national policy of cooperating with other nations.

**interventionism**  Interference in the economic or political affairs of another nation.

**isolationism**  A national policy of refusing to become involved in political alliances or economic relations with other nations.

# For Further Reading

Brown, Gene. *The Struggle to Grow: Expansionism and Industrialization (1880-1913)*. New York: Twenty-First Century Books, 1993.

Dolan, Edward F. *Panama and the United States: Their Canal, Their Stormy Years*. New York: Franklin Watts, 1990.

Faber, Doris, and Harold Faber. *American Government: Great Lives*. New York: Scribners, 1988.

Foner, Eric, and John A. Garraty, editors. *The Reader's Companion to American History*. Boston: Houghton Mifflin, 1991.

Nixon, Richard. *Seize the Moment: America's Challenge in a One-Superpower World*. New York: Simon and Schuster, 1992.

Pascoe, Elaine. *Neighbors at Odds: U.S. Policy in Latin America*. New York: Franklin Watts, 1990.

Polesetsky, Matthew, and William Dudley, editors. *The New World Order: Opposing Viewpoints*. San Diego, CA: Greenhaven Press, Inc., 1991.

Steins, Richard. *The Postwar Years: The Cold War and the Atomic Age (1950-1959)*. New York: Twenty-First Century Books, 1993.

# Source Notes

"A Letter From Sarajevo." *Time*. December 12, 1994.

Barnes, Fred. "Parting Shots." *The New Republic*. February 8, 1993.

Bragdon, Henry W., Samuel P. McCutchen, and Donald A. Richie. *A History of a Free Nation*. Lake Forest, IL: Macmillan/McGraw-Hill, 1992.

Church, George J. "Destination Haiti." *Time*. September 26, 1994.

Desmond, Edward W. "If the Shooting Starts, Who Would Win?" *Time*. April 4, 1994.

"Duty, Honor, Fruits and Vegetables." *Time*. November 29, 1993.

Faber, Doris, and Harold Faber. *American Government: Great Lives*. New York: Scribners, 1988.

Fedarko, Kevin. "Bad Blood and Broken Promises." *Time*. December 26, 1994.

_____. "Getting the Hang of It." *Time*. December 12, 1994.

Fukuyama, Francis. "The Beginning of Foreign Policy." *The New Republic*. August 17, 1992.

Grunwald, Harry. "Letter to an Isolationist." *Time*. November 8, 1993.

"Heroes." *People*. December 1994-January 1995.

Hofstadter, Richard, and Beatrice K. Hofstadter. *Great Issues in American History*. New York: Random House, 1982.

"Into Africa." *The New Republic*. December 28, 1992.

Kramer, Michael. "In Search of the Clinton Doctrine." *Time*. October 11, 1993.

_____. "It's All Foreign to Clinton." *Time*. October 18, 1993.

_____. "The Case for Intervention." *Time*. September 26, 1994.

Krauthammer, Charles. "The Greatest Cold War Myth of All." *Time*. November 29, 1993.

_____. "Bob Dole's Bosnia Folly." *Time*. December 12, 1994.

McAllister, J.F.O. "Somalia: When to Stay, When to Go." *Time*. October 4, 1993.

_____. "The Koreas: Frightening Face-Off." *Time*. December 13, 1993.

Morison, Samuel Eliot, Henry Steel Commager, and William E. Leuchtenburg. *The Growth of the American Republic*. Seventh Edition. New York: Oxford University Press, 1980.

Nixon, Richard. *Seize the Moment: America's Challenge in a One-Superpower World*. New York: Simon and Schuster, 1992.

Ogden, Christopher. "Scrooge Goes Abroad." *Time*. December 19, 1994.

Reilly, John E., ed. *American Public Opinion and U.S. Foreign Policy 1991*. Chicago: The Chicago Council on Foreign Relations, 1991.

Steel, Ronald. "Beyond Interventionism: Mission Control." *The New Republic*. January 25, 1993.

Thompson, Mark. "Going Up, Up in Arms." *Time*. December 12, 1994.

_____. "Diplomacy: Well, A Nuke Or Two." *Time*. April 11, 1994.

Walsh, James. "Allied in Failure." *Time*. December 12, 1994.

Wright, Robert. "Bold Old Vision." *The New Republic*. January 25, 1993.

_____. "Good Ghali." *The New Republic*. August 15, 1994.

# Index

**Photo Credits**
Cover: ©Department of Defense/Gamma Liaison; p. 4: ©Steve Lehman/SABA; pp. 7, 12, 15: North Wind Picture
Archives; pp. 9, 10, 28, 34, 36, 41, 49, 57, 58: AP/Wide World Photos; pp. 17, 23: The Bettmann Archive; pp. 19, 20:
Library of Congress; pp. 26, 27, 33, 35, 39: UPI/Bettmann; pp. 30, 42, 44: ©Gamma Liaison; p. 47: ©Michael
Abramson; p. 52: ©Renato Rotolo/Gamma Liaison; p. 53: ©P. Breese/Gamma Liaison; p. 54: ©Shawn Henry/SABA.
Graphs by Blackbirch Graphics, Inc.